Note to parents, carers and teachers

Read it yourself is a series of modern stories, favourite characters, traditional tales and first reference books written in a simple way for children who are learning to read. The books can be read independently or as part of a guided reading session.

Each book is carefully structured to include many high-frequency words vital for first reading. The sentences on each page are supported closely by pictures to help with understanding, and to offer lively details to talk about.

The books are graded into four levels that progressively introduce wider vocabulary and longer text as a reader's ability and confidence grows.

Ideas for use

• Begin by looking through the book and talking about the pictures. Has your child heard this story or looked at this subject before?

• Help your child with any words he does not know, either by helping him to sound them out or supplying them yourself.

• Developing readers can be concentrating so hard on the words that they sometimes don't fully grasp the meaning of what they're reading. Answering the quiz questions at the end of the book will help with understanding.

For more information and advice on Read it yourself and book banding, visit **www.ladybird.com/readityourself**

Book
Band
6

Level 2 is ideal for children who have received some reading instruction and can read short, simple sentences with help.

Special features:

Frequent repetition of subject words and concepts

Short, simple sentences

Careful match between text and pictures

Large, clear labels and captions

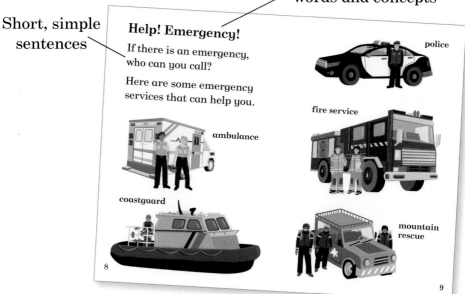

Help! Emergency!

If there is an emergency, who can you call?

Here are some emergency services that can help you.

police

fire service

ambulance

coastguard

mountain rescue

8

9

The fire service

Firefighters come to help when there is a fire.

They get into their fire engine and rush to the fire.

The firefighters put out the fire with water from their fire engine.

firefighter

fire engine

10

11

Educational Consultant: Geraldine Taylor
Book Banding Consultant: Kate Ruttle
Subject Consultant: Chris Woodford

LADYBIRD BOOKS

UK | USA | Canada | Ireland | Australia
India | New Zealand | South Africa

Ladybird Books is part of the Penguin Random House group of companies
whose addresses can be found at global.penguinrandomhouse.com.

www.penguin.co.uk   www.puffin.co.uk   www.ladybird.co.uk

Penguin
Random House
UK

First published 2016
This edition 2019
001

Copyright © Ladybird Books Ltd, 2016

Printed in China

A CIP catalogue record for this book is available from the British Library

ISBN: 978-0-241-40540-6

All correspondence to:
Ladybird Books
Penguin Random House Children's
80 Strand, London WC2R 0RL

Emergency Rescue

Written by Catherine Baker
Illustrated by Jenna Riggs

Contents

Help! Emergency!

If there is an emergency, who can you call?

Here are some emergency services that can help you.

ambulance

coastguard

police

fire service

mountain
rescue

The fire service

Firefighters come to help when there is a fire.

They get into their fire engine and rush to the fire.

fire engine

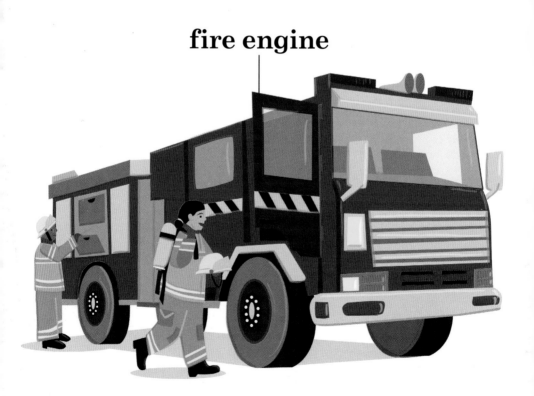

The firefighters put out the fire with water from their fire engine.

firefighter

Firefighters can help

Firefighters help when there is an accident, too.

firefighters

13

The police help people

If there is an emergency or a crime, the police can help.

police

There has been a crime. The police are here to help the people.

crime

15

Look out for trouble

The police have helicopters that help them to look out for trouble, too.

accident

police helicopter

This police helicopter has seen an accident. It puts out a call for help.

17

The ambulance service

When people are hurt in an accident, they call for an ambulance.

The ambulance will rush to take them to hospital.

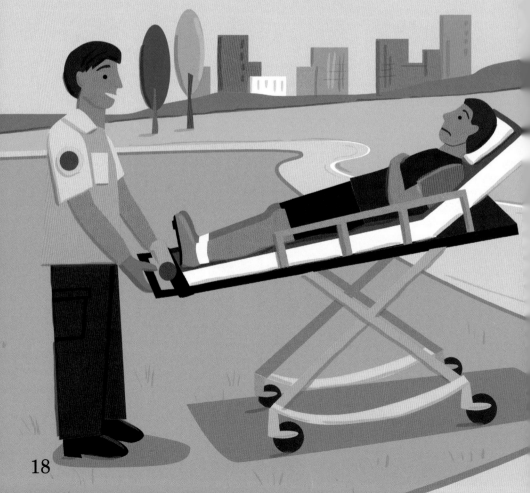

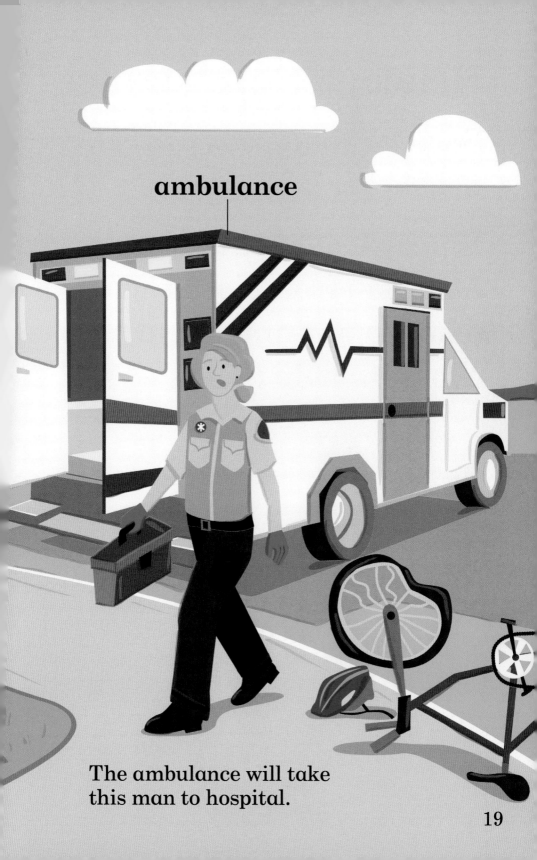

ambulance

The ambulance will take
this man to hospital.

Helicopter ambulances

Some ambulances are helicopters!

If people get hurt a very long way from hospital, a helicopter ambulance comes to help them.

helicopter ambulance

This man is hurt. The helicopter
has seen him!

Emergency at sea!

If you are in trouble out at sea, who can help you?

The coastguard!

The coastguard rescues people who are hurt or in trouble at sea.

coastguard

This man is in trouble.

Boats and helicopters

Coastguards have boats
and helicopters to help
people in trouble.

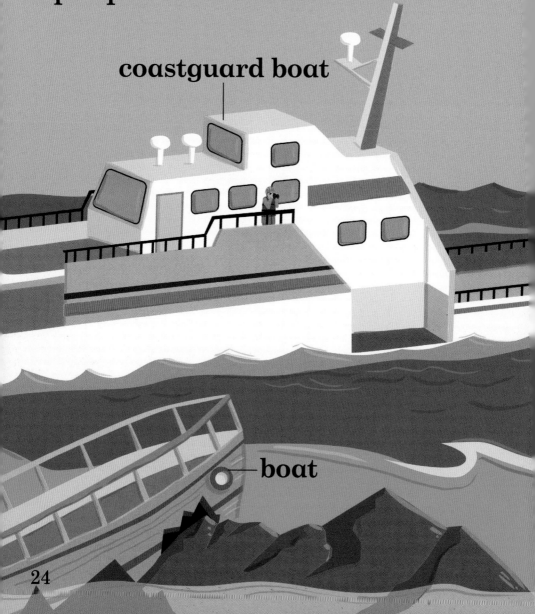

coastguard boat

boat

coastguard helicopter

This man is hurt, but the helicopter can get him out of the water.

The coastguard will rescue the people from here.

Mountain rescue

Some people get into trouble on the mountains. They are a very long way from a hospital!

But the mountain rescue service is here to help them.

helicopter

A mountain rescue helicopter helps with this emergency.

Picture glossary

 accident

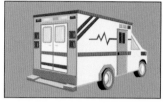 ambulance

 boat

 car

 coastguard

 fire engine

 firefighter

 helicopter

 mountain rescue

 police

 police car

Index

Emergency Rescue quiz

What have you learnt about Emergency Rescue? Answer these questions and find out!

- How do firefighters rush to a fire or an accident?

- Who comes to help if there is a crime?

- When is a helicopter ambulance used?

- Who rescues people at sea?

www.ladybird.com